Building Kites

Flying High with Math

Building Kites
Flying High with Math

Nancy Ann Belsky

Dale Seymour Publications

Nancy Belsky first published her sled-kite lesson as "Kites, Kites, Kites: Classroom Activities—Measuring, Making, and Flying!" in *The Elementary Mathematician* (Spring 1992): 1–15. The sled-kite lesson is presented in this book courtesy of COMAP, Lexington, Massachusetts.

Project Editor: Joan Gideon
Production: Claire Flaherty
Art: Carl Yoshihara
Cover Design: Rachel Gage
Text Design: Lisa Raine

Published by Dale Seymour Publications, an imprint of the Alternative Publishing Group of Addison-Wesley Publishing Company.

Order Number DS21353
ISBN 0-86651-918-1

7 8 9 10 MA 02 01

DALE
SEYMOUR
PUBLICATIONS
P.O. BOX 10888
PALO ALTO, CA 94303

This book is printed on recycled paper.

Contents

Introduction

Kids and kites are a natural combination for hands-on involvement in the middle-school mathematics classroom. Kites fire the imagination and are always met with enthusiasm by students. Kite building and flying give students an opportunity to solve math problems while working together to build something creative. They learn to follow written directions and experience the satisfaction of seeing their kites fly successfully. Students use math not only to build their kites, but also to estimate the height of their kite in flight. This book presents four kite designs your students can build. Each design is accompanied by a lesson plan, student directions, and worksheets for mathematics lessons that you can use to teach or reinforce the math skills involved in making the kites.

A good way to begin a kite unit is to describe anecdotes from the history of kites. Some of these anecdotes are presented in the section "Kites Through the Ages" (pages 7–8). A page of history is also included at the beginning of each kite unit. You may want to duplicate these pages and give them to the students as you begin a new unit. Provide your students with other resources on the history of kites or ask them to do their own research about kites and share it with the class.

To create successful kites, students must cooperate. Because sheath-style box kites and tetrahedral kites are large and take a lot of work, only one kite per group of four students is suggested. The sled and flat-style box kites are less difficult to make and every student can make his or her own kite, or students can work in pairs. When grouping students, try to balance their abilities so they will complement each other's skills.

Students often have difficulty following directions. These lessons are designed to minimize student dependence on the teacher. After an introduction or demonstration, students work cooperatively and independently from their own copies of the directions. They will be developing the necessary life skill of following written directions.

While the students are working, circulate around the room asking and answering questions. If you make a sample kite before presenting the lesson to the class, you will be better prepared to answer the students' questions and anticipate potential problems. (Your kite can also be used as a sample if you feel your class needs a model— some classes can succeed without the prototype.) Students should be allowed to ask you questions only if every person in their group is unable to answer the question. Students often do not read the directions carefully and rely only on the pictures. When students ask a question that is addressed in the directions, encourage them to reread the directions out loud and restate, in their own words, what they are to do.

Students will learn valuable skills as they make patterns out of inexpensive material (such as newsprint, butcher paper, or large rolls of graph paper) before cutting the more expensive material for the sail. The lesson "Blowing Up Rectangles" (page 19) prepares them to enlarge the pattern uniformly.

Taking to the sky and flying high is a fitting way to end a unit. Students can see the success of their kites—they have applied mathematics to real problems and produced a kite that will fly. Students also learn to estimate the height of kites in flight, giving them a way to evaluate their skills at kite making and flying.

Display your students' kites by hanging them from the ceiling in the classroom, library, or hallway. Your kite show will create eye-catching proof that math is a high-flying subject.

Materials and Equipment for Making Kites

The materials used for kites must be both light and strong. The materials listed below are in order from weakest to strongest. Generally, the stronger materials should be used for larger kites. Cost must also be considered when working in the classroom. Suggested materials and alternatives will also be included in each lesson.

Materials for Sails

Paper

This inexpensive material is readily available in most schools.

Tissue paper is light but is not strong and tears easily; this can make it difficult to work with. Tissue paper comes in many colors and makes impressive kites. It is appropriate for small kites and for covering cells in tetrahedral kites. Tissue-paper kites tear easily when flying, and should not be flown when the grass is wet.

Newsprint is inexpensive, readily available, and comes in many widths. Students can decorate it with marker, paint, or crayon. Newsprint can be used for patterns and for small or medium-size kites.

Roll graph paper makes an excellent material for patterns and can be used for kites as well. The lines of the graph paper help students make patterns with square corners.

Roll paper comes in rolls 36" wide. Most schools have several colors available for covering bulletin boards. Students can decorate roll paper with marker, crayon, or paint, or cut sections of a kite from different colors and tape them together for an interesting effect. Roll paper is appropriate for small and medium-size kites.

(Construction paper is too brittle to be effective as kite material and too heavy to fly well. Kites made of construction paper should be made for decoration only.)

Plastic

Plastic is strong, light, and will hold together when the ground is wet from dew or a recent rain. Most plastic can be decorated with permanent markers. Decoration on clear plastic produces an interesting effect.

Trash bags come in different sizes, colors, and thicknesses (bags less than one mil thick can be difficult to work with because they are too thin; trash-compactor bags are generally too heavy to fly well). Slit the bags open to trace the kite pattern, or use them whole or in sections to cover cells for box kites.

Drop cloths can be found in the paint department of many hardware stores. Several kites can be cut from one drop cloth.

Spunbonded olefin

Products such as Tyvek™, made of spunbonded olefin, are excellent materials for kites because they are tear-resistant, stronger than paper, and less expensive than fabric. Buy them by the yard from kite-supply catalogues and in 100-foot rolls from building-supply stores. A roll is long enough to make dozens of kites.

Fabric

Choose a fabric with a close weave. When cutting and piecing, consider the grain of the fabric. The seams for the dowel supports should be with the grain. When making the pattern for a fabric kite, remember to add allowances for hemming the edges.

Ripstop nylon, the best kite material available, is lightweight, strong, and rip-resistant. It comes in a variety of colors that can be pieced together or appliquéd for striking effects. Ripstop nylon can be purchased in most fabric stores and ordered from kite-supply catalogues. It may be cut out with a thin-tipped soldering iron. The heat melts the thread ends, so hemming is not necessary.

Kite sails can also be made from other fabrics, including cotton or inexpensive types of nylon such as taffeta. Although these don't have the tear resistance of ripstop nylon, they come in a variety of weaves, weights, colors, and patterns—students can create interesting effects through piecing and appliqué.

Materials for Spars

Spar materials must be light and strong. The size of your kite is limited by the length of your spars.

Drinking straws

Use straws in small and miniature kites and as a frame for multicelled tetrahedral kites.

Dowels

Dowels are available in hardware, hobby, and building-supply stores in several thicknesses starting at $\frac{1}{8}$". They come in lengths of 36" and 48".

Aluminum tubing, fiberglass rods, and graphite tubing

These strong, lightweight materials are all available from kite-supply houses, but their cost is prohibitive for most school programs.

Plastic tubing

Tubing, sold in hardware stores by the foot, is used to connect dowel spars. It is sized by the inner diameter, or ID. The ID should match the diameter of the dowel. For example, $\frac{3}{16}$" dowels recommended for the box kite are connected with $\frac{3}{16}$" ID tubing. Plastic tubing is available in hardware and building-supply stores. Pet stores carry $\frac{1}{8}$" ID plastic tubing for air pumps.

Materials for Tails and Streamers

Tails stabilize and balance a kite and enhance its design. Although the kites in this book can fly tailless, students enjoy adding the colorful touch of tails to their creations. The friction of the wind blowing over the tail helps keep the kite upright by adding drag and increasing the surface area.

Paper

Though paper is inexpensive and colorful, it must be kept dry and handled carefully. Crepe paper streamers come in a wide variety of vivid colors. The weight of crepe paper makes it appropriate for medium and large kites. For smaller kites, strips of tissue paper may be used.

Plastic

Plastic is inexpensive, flexible, does not easily rip, and is not weakened by water. Strips cut from plastic bags make good tails. Lay the unopened bag on a desk and cut crosswise through all layers at one-inch intervals. Open the strips and cut the tails to the desired length.

Surveyor's tape

This lightweight plastic is an inexpensive source of colorful tails. It is sold in building-supply and hardware stores in rolls one inch wide and 150–200 feet long.

Ribbon

Ribbon comes in a wide variety of colors, weights, and materials. Be sure to match the weight of the ribbon to the kite. Cloth ribbon such as grosgrain or satin should be used only for large kites; gift-wrapping ribbon makes good tails for medium-size kites, and curling ribbon is excellent for small, light kites.

String for Flying Kites

The weight of the string used to fly a kite must fit the kite—the larger the kite, the stronger the string must be. If the string is too heavy, it will weigh the kite down, and the kite will not fly properly. When using heavy string, wear gloves to protect your hands.

Thread (crochet, button)

Thread is appropriate for small kites.

Household string

String is light and strong. It usually comes in 300-foot rolls. The end of the string is often not tied to the spool, so warn students to be cautious when the string is almost played out, or the kite will take off to points unknown.

Fishing line

Though used by some people to fly kites, it is not recommended for school use because it will not break when tangled. It is dangerous to wildlife and to students caught in it.

Kite string

String made specifically for kites in many test weights is available through kite-supply houses. Made of braided Dacron, it is usually too expensive for general classroom use. It is needed for large or strong-pulling kites and should only be used while wearing gloves.

Adhesives

Generally, any glue or tape that is normally used on a material can be used with that material when making kites.

Glue

Glue sticks are easy to handle and dry fast. They work on all weights of paper, including tissue paper.

White glue is excellent for gluing most paper to paper and to dowels. It must be allowed to dry thoroughly before flying the kite. White glue is difficult to use on tissue paper.

Glue guns are excellent for gluing spunbonded olefin and cloth to dowels. They can also glue cloth to cloth with reasonable results. One or two glue guns may be shared in a cooperative classroom. When students are allowed to use glue guns, supervision must be provided and safety precautions stressed. Hot glue guns tend to melt most plastics.

Tapes

Cellophane tape is appropriate for small to medium-size paper kites. It can be used to tape dowels to small plastic kites as well. When working on small kites, remember that excessive amounts of tape can change the weight and balance of the kite.

Masking tape works well for joining medium and heavy papers. Masking tape is also appropriate for taping spars to the kite body in medium-size paper, plastic, and spunbonded olefin kites.

Strapping tape is the best adhesive for medium and large kites made of plastic and spunbonded olefin. It is used to tape the kite body to the spars. Strapping tape is very sticky, so designate which classroom scissors students should use to cut it. Nail polish remover can be used to remove the sticky deposit that develops on the scissors.

Sewing

Students can sew cloth kites together by hand or machine. Machine sewing can be done with parents at home, or in cooperation with the home economics department at school.

Equipment and Storage

Most of the equipment you need is readily available. Store it in an out-of-the-way location, such as the back of the room or in a closet, and bring it out only when it is needed. The equipment containers suggested here are available in most schools at no cost.

Scissors

Most of the materials used in these lessons can be cut with regular classroom scissors. If fabric scissors are available, be sure to instruct the students not to use them to score dowels for breaking or to cut strapping tape. Tie a ribbon to the handle of the scissors to remind students to use them only on fabric. Scissors may be stored point down in a number-ten can, often available from the school kitchen.

Skill knives

Use skill knives to score or cut dowels. Place a board under the dowel when cutting to protect the surface of desks or counters. Because of the potential for misuse, store skill knives in your pocket and allow students to use them only under close supervision.

Yardsticks or meter sticks

One yardstick or meter stick per group is required for making patterns and measuring materials. They may be stored on end in a clean trash can or an empty five-gallon pail. Dowels, grouped by size and held together with elastic bands, may also be stored in the same trash can or bucket.

Rulers

You need a classroom set of rulers for measuring patterns and materials. They may be stored on end in number-ten cans.

Squares

Both T squares and L squares are useful for checking square corners on patterns or kites, but they are not essential. They can often be borrowed from industrial-arts classrooms. If squares are not available, show students that books have 90° corners, which can also be used to check for right angles.

Needles

Needles with eyes large enough to hold kite string are used for bridling the kites and for threading string through straws. Embroidery, crewel, and yarn needles are all appropriate. Canisters for 35mm film make good needle containers. A piece of string left in the eye of the needle, makes it easier to locate.

Markers

Both permanent and washable markers are used for decorating the kites. Only permanent markers work on spunbonded olefin and plastic. Markers may be stored in a shoe box or number-ten can.

Goggles

To protect the students' eyes when they construct the box kites, borrow goggles from the science or industrial-arts department.

Keeping Track of Equipment

Use an accounting system to keep track of equipment. Number each piece of equipment with a permanent marker or masking tape, and assign each group a corresponding number. For example, group three gets scissors, tape, meter stick, and rulers identified by a 3. At the end of class, you can easily determine the group responsible for a missing item.

Kites Through the Ages

Kites have been around for at least 2,000 years, probably originating in China. Throughout the ages people have flown kites as part of religious celebrations, in competitions, and for pleasure. They have also used kites for construction, transportation, military, and scientific purposes.

A Victory Without Bloodshed

According to Chinese legend, about 2,000 years ago during the Han dynasty, kites saved the kingdom from invading barbarians. The emperor's advisor instructed him to attach bamboo pipes to kites and fly them over the enemy camp on a moonless night. The wind blowing through the pipes made an eerie sound. The emperor then sent infiltrators into the camp to spread the word that the noise was that of ghosts proclaiming the coming defeat of the invaders. As a result, the invaders were so scared they left in a hurry.

An Electrifying Experience

Benjamin Franklin was always fascinated by kites. He wrote that when he was a boy he had used a kite to pull himself across a pond while floating on his back. He also used kites for scientific experiments. In 1752, he flew a kite in a lightning storm to prove that lightning was a natural phenomenon called electricity. This experiment led to the invention of the lightning rod, which has saved many buildings and lives over the years. When

Franklin wrote about the results of his experiment, he included clear directions with detailed safety precautions. Nonetheless, shortly after Franklin's work was published, a Swedish scientist died while trying to duplicate the experiment.

The Original Horseless Carriage

One of the most interesting examples of the use of kites as pulling devices was developed around 1825 by an English schoolteacher named George Pocock. He invented a lightweight, kite-drawn vehicle, which he named a *charvolant*. This carriage was pulled by two 8-foot-high kites flown on one towing line. The kites were flown very high to catch the strong winds. Pocock used a four-line bridle, which gave him enough control over the kites to fly them almost into the wind. The carriage drawn by his kite could carry five people and reach speeds of 20 to 25 mph—a speed almost unheard of in his time. Pocock also believed kites could lift people. To demonstrate this, he seated his son and daughter in chairs and lifted them high in the air with kites. He imagined kites could be used in this manner to rescue shipwrecked sailors from the sea.

A Spy in the Sky

Before the invention of airplanes, military forces from many countries attempted to raise men by kite to observe enemy forces. One interesting personality who worked on military applications of kites was

Samuel Franklin Cody. Born in Texas, Cody was a cowboy who may have learned to build and fly kites from a Chinese cook. Cody traveled all over the United States in a wild-West show, and his audiences often confused him with Buffalo Bill (William Cody). After marrying an Englishwoman, he settled in England in 1890. There he spent an increasing amount of time experimenting with kites, while continuing his career as a showman and incorporating his interest in kites into his exhibitions. He designed a double-celled box kite with wings that successfully raised people into the air.

In 1906, after considering Cody's projects for a few years, the British War Office began using his kite designs for military observation. Cody invented a system of military observation, in which a kite raised an observer in a basket with a telescope, camera, and gun. Notes were sent to and from the ground to relay information. In this way, an army could track enemy movements from the air. Cody became an officer in the British army and was named chief kite instructor. Cody continued to work on manned flight. In 1908 he became the first person in England to build and fly an airplane. He died on August 7, 1913, while testing one of his own waterplanes. He left behind a fascinating legacy of kite and airplane designs.

Though the airplane made the use of kites for military observation obsolete, kites continued to have military value in the early twentieth century. They were flown around military establishments to keep out spy planes. The strings and wires attached to the kites might shear off an airplane's wing or entangle a propeller.

Flying kites near airfields and in flight patterns is still prohibited because of the danger kite string poses to aircraft.

What Will the Weather Be?

William Eddy, a journalist from Bayone, New Jersey, developed one of today's most popular kites. Eddy wanted to lift photographic and meteorological equipment, and he needed a stable, reliable kite with good pulling ability. Eddy began to develop his kite in 1893 as an adaptation of the two-stick bowed kite that has been flown in Malaysia and Indonesia for centuries. He improved his design while working with weather observers at the Blue Hill Observatory in Massachusetts. Eddy was granted a patent on the Eddy Kite in 1900. By flying more than one kite on the same string in trains, Eddy gained more lift. Because Eddy Kites fly without a tail, it is easier to fly a train of them. Kites similar to this are still used today for science and recreation.

Using Kites to Solve Problems

People have designed kites to solve many problems: to pull boats across bodies of water, to facilitate aerial photography, to raise meteorological instruments for the study of the weather. A kite was used to begin construction of the suspension bridge just below Niagara Falls in New York state. The kite was flown across the river; then thicker and thicker ropes were pulled across on the kite string. Finally cables were pulled over, enabling the construction to begin. Kites are currently being used for wind prospecting to determine the best locations to erect wind-powered electric generators.

The Sled Kite

The sled kite consists of a canopy or sail and two keels to which the bridle is tied. It is easy to make and flies well in light, steady winds.

The first sled kite, known as the *Allison Sled*, was invented by William M. Allison. Allison was born in Canada and moved to Dayton, Ohio. He liked to fly kites with children and began to experiment with his own designs. In 1950 he invented a flexible, or semirigid, kite. It featured a tapered end and its spars extended only along its length. In 1956, his application for a patent on this kite was approved.

In the early 1960s, Frank Scott modified Allison's sled kites. He added a vent and made the spars parallel. He called it a *sled* because it was a *Flexible Flyer*, which was the brand name of the snow sleds that most children used at that time. Both Allison, the man who invented this form of kite, and Scott, the man who improved and popularized it, lived in Dayton, Ohio, the home of the Wright brothers.

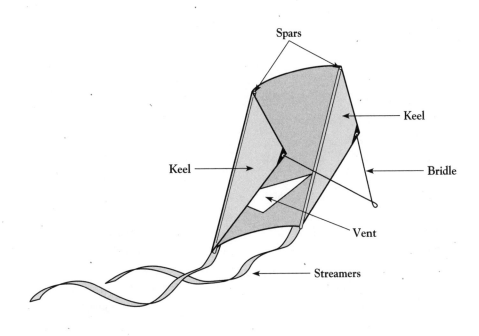

Sled Kite Lesson Plan

Objectives

- to make a kite that flies
- to develop measuring skills
- to explore what happens to the area of a rectangle when both dimensions are multiplied by the same number
- to work with another student to solve a mathematical problem
- to follow instructions
- to explore balance through symmetry in kite making and flying

Materials

- $\frac{1}{8}$" by 48" hardwood dowels—one per student (plus extras in case of breakage)
- kite sail material—plastic trash bags, spunbonded olefin, paper
- streamers—surveyor's tape or plastic bag strips
- string for bridling
- kite string
- tape—strapping tape (for plastic or spunbonded olefin sails) or masking tape (for plastic or paper sails)
- newsprint, roll graph paper, or other large paper for patterns
- copies of small pattern (one for each pair of students, page 15)
- copies of "Directions for Making a Sled Kite" (one per student, page 14)
- copies of "The Sled Kite" (page 9, optional)
- copies of "Measuring 1" and "Measuring 2" (pages 17–18, optional)
- copies of "Blowing Up Rectangles" (pages 20–21, optional)

Equipment

- yardsticks or meter sticks
- T square, L square, or other 90° angle
- scissors
- permanent markers
- needles with large eyes
- overhead transparency of small kite pattern (page 15)
- clear plastic ruler for the overhead

Introduction

Discuss Allison's development of the sled kite and Scott's adaptations. Explain that the sled doesn't look like most kites, but it flies very well if the directions for making it are followed correctly.

Class Preparation

Students should know how to measure and enlarge a pattern. Suggested preactivity exercises are "Measuring 1" and "Measuring 2" and "Blowing Up Rectangles."

Making the Full-Size Pattern

Copy the small pattern of the kite onto an overhead transparency and project it onto the screen. Demonstrate to the whole class how to measure the dimensions of the kite pattern. Explain that unless they want a 6" by 8" kite, the pattern must be enlarged. When a pattern is enlarged, each dimension must be multiplied *by the same number* to get the correct proportions. Use the number three as an example, multiplying the length and width of the pattern by three so that the final kite will measure 18" high by 24" wide. Make a rectangle 18" by 24". Point out that the spar (dowel) will be 18" long. Show the class that there are only six points they need to identify to draw the outline of the kite. Find these points on your pattern, and then demonstrate how to connect the points to form the outline of the pattern.

Group students in twos or threes for this lesson. Give each group one set of directions, one pattern, rulers and a yardstick, and enough large paper for the full-size pattern. Tell students the dimensions of the available trash bags and limit each student to one 48-inch dowel. The groups will have to decide how large a kite can be made from the available materials. A pair of students may choose to make their kites both the same size (24"), to make two different-size kites (for example, 30" and 18"), or to combine their resources to make a kite 48" tall. At this point the groups can begin to work independently at their own pace. Circulate around the room asking questions and supplying an extra hand when needed. Allow students to problem solve as a group. As each group completes their pattern(s), check their work for accuracy. (See the troubleshooting section at the end of the lesson plan for solutions to common errors.)

Creating Vents

Once students have made a sled kite with the standard vent, they may want to individualize their kites by varying the shape of the vent. The vents must be cut from the lower third of the kite. The area of the vents should be one-fourth the area of this lower third section. When these factors are taken into account, the kite will usually fly well.

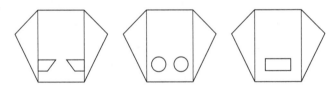

Making the Sail

When a group has completed their full-size pattern(s), give them the materials they need for the sail. They should trace their pattern onto the material before cutting. (Ballpoint pen and permanent marker will draw on plastic.) From this point on, expect groups to follow the written instructions with little help. If students need help understanding the directions, they should ask others in the group; they are allowed to come to the teacher only if no one can help them. See the troubleshooting section at the end of the lesson plan for common errors to check for when looking at students' work.

Attaching the Spars

The dowels must be cut to the length of the spar. Tape the dowels onto the sail at the points indicated on the directions. Instruct the students to fold long pieces of tape over the top and bottom of the sail to keep the spars in place.

Bridling

Select the first group that reaches this point in the lesson, and demonstrate how to bridle the kite. This group will become the class "experts" in bridling. As other groups reach this point, send them to the expert group for help.

There are two ways to attach the bridle to the end of the keels.

- Reinforce the point of each keel with strapping tape. (The threads in the tape should go in a vertical direction.) Make a hole in each keel with a hole punch. Put the ends of the bridle through the holes.

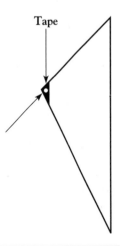

Tape

- Make an overhand knot in a 6" piece of string to form a loop. Put a 2" piece of strapping tape through the loop and fold it over the end of the outer angle of the keel.

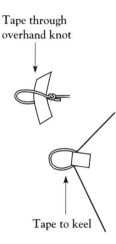

Tape through
overhand knot

Tape to keel

Cut a piece of string for the bridle that is four times the length of the distance between spars. Attach the ends of the bridle to the angle of the keel. Fold the string in half and make an overhand loop in the middle of the bridle. Attach the flying string to this loop.

Attaching Tails

Show the second group to finish bridling their kite how to measure and attach the streamers, or tails. This group will become the "experts" on tails. Stress that the kite will not fly upright unless the streamers are identical in length and taped symmetrically. Tails should be attached with tape at the base of the spars. Students often double the streamers for a decorative effect. They should be aware that if the tails weigh too much, they will hold down the kite. Adjustments to the tails are often made in the field where kites are tested. Students will be using trial and error to make their kites fly in the best form.

Troubleshooting

Nonsquare corner

Students often have difficulty with their patterns because the corners are not square. If a carpenter's square is available, teach the students to use it. If not, they can use the corner of a book to trace the corner, and then use a yardstick to extend the sides to the correct length.

Vent in wrong third of kite

One common error in the pattern occurs when students place the vent in the upper third of the kite. This will inhibit rather then facilitate air flow.

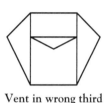

Vent in wrong third

One keel upside down

When plastic of various colors is available, students will often cut the flaps and the body of the sail out of different colors to make their kites more interesting. A common mistake is to tape one keel on upside down. This will make the kite dip wildly in flight. Students with spatial-orientation problems sometimes put a keel upside down when making the pattern.

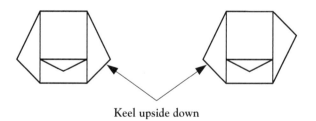

Keel upside down

Variations in Materials

Tissue paper

Small sled kites may be made with tissue-paper sails and drinking-straw spars. Curling ribbon makes attractive streamers. This variation flies well in very light wind or when students run. These kites are attractive projects because tissue paper and curling ribbon come in many colors.

Fabric

Very attractive sled kites can be made from lightweight, closely woven fabric. Look in the section on materials (pages 3–4) for suggestions. Students can make casings for the spars from single-fold bias binding that is sewn onto the fabric and secured at the bottom to keep the spar from sliding out. Fabric ribbons make excellent streamers for this kite.

Directions for Making a Sled Kite

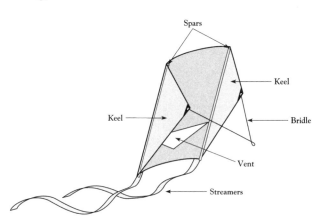

You need these materials:

- sail material—paper or plastic
- pattern material—paper
- $\frac{3}{16}$" or $\frac{1}{8}$" dowel—two dowels per kite
- tape
- string

Put a check in each box as you complete the step.

☐ Make your pattern. Decide what size you want your kite to be. Measure the lengths of the sides of the kite on your pattern. Enlarge the size of the pattern by multiplying each length by the same number. Draw your full-sized pattern on paper.

☐ Make the sail. Use your pattern to trace the sail on paper or plastic, and then cut it out, including the vent.

☐ Attach the dowels. Cut two pieces of $\frac{1}{8}$" dowel the length of the spar. If your sail is taller than 30", use $\frac{3}{16}$" dowels and add a third dowel parallel to the spars down the middle. Tape the dowels to the kite at the tape marks. Make sure the tape goes over the ends of the dowels to the back of the kite.

☐ Decorate your kite.

☐ Make the bridle. Cut a bridle of kite string four times the distance from one dowel to the other. Reinforce the kite material with strapping tape at the points of the keels, marked on the pattern with triangles. Attach the bridle to the keels at these points. Tie an overhand loop in the middle of the bridle to attach flying string.

☐ Add the streamers. Cut two tails for stability; each tail should be three times the length of the diagonal of the kite's body. Tape tails to the base of the dowels as shown.

☐ Attach string to the bridle loop. It's ready to fly.

© Dale Seymour Publications

Pattern for Sled Kite

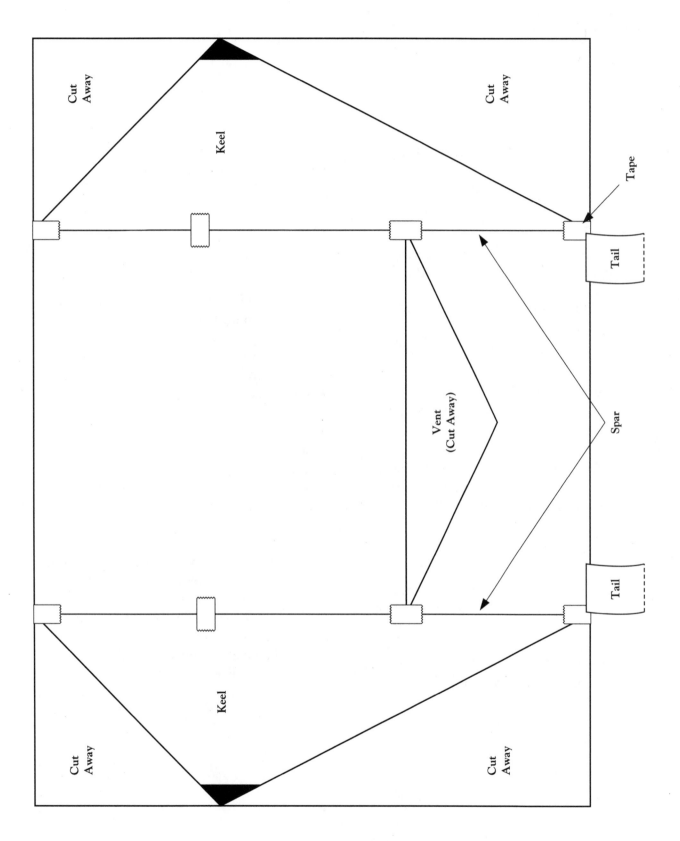

Measuring Lesson Plan

Objectives
- to be able to round measurements to the nearest unit
- to review measuring skills

Equipment
- rulers marked in $\frac{1}{8}$" increments (one per group)
- nine items of different lengths labeled 1 through 9
- copies of "Measuring 1" and "Measuring 2" (one per group, pages 17–18)
- ruler for the overhead projector (optional)

Class Preparation
Collect nine items of different lengths, and number them. Set up nine centers that the groups will circulate through to measure the items. Make a chart similar to "Measuring 1" on the overhead projector or board, naming the items and leaving room for the length of the item.

Introduction
Group the students in threes and pass out "Measuring 1." Direct each group to measure all nine items. One person will be the measurer, one the checker, and one the recorder. They can switch jobs at each station. Do not answer any questions such as, "Should we round off?" or "How accurate should our measurement be?"

Discussing Results
When all groups have measured each item, bring the class together to discuss the results. Record each group's measurement of each item on the class chart. There should be different measurements for some of the items. Discuss these questions.
- Which is the correct measurement?
- Can there be more than one correct measurement for the same item? (Yes, if the measurement is rounded off to a different increment. For example, if an item is $7\frac{3}{8}$" long, it is 7" when rounding to the nearest inch, but $7\frac{1}{2}$" if rounded to the nearest half inch.)
- Which measurement is most appropriate to use?
- When is it appropriate to use a measurement to the nearest inch? (When measuring long items or when a more accurate measurement is not needed.)
- When is it appropriate to measure to the nearest $\frac{1}{16}$"? (When measuring small items or when an accurate measurement is needed.)

Demonstrate on the overhead projector how to measure one or two items to the nearest inch, half inch, and quarter inch. Distribute "Measuring 2" and ask the groups to remeasure each item to the indicated approximation.

When the groups are finished, compare answers again. There should be little disagreement.

Measuring 1

With your partners, measure the item at each work station. Fill in
the name of the item and the length.

Station	Item	Length
1		
2		
3		
4		
5		
6		
7		
8		
9		

Measuring 2

With your partners, measure the item at each work station. Fill in the name of the item and record the measurement to the nearest inch, $\frac{1}{2}$ inch, and $\frac{1}{4}$ inch.

Station	Item	Inch	Length $\frac{1}{2}$ Inch	$\frac{1}{4}$ Inch
1				
2				
3				
4				
5				
6				
7				
8				
9				

Blowing Up Rectangles Lesson Plan

When enlarging patterns, students are often surprised that the overall size of the kite is much larger than expected. These activities will help them understand the difference between arithmetic progression and geometric progression. Students should be familiar with the concept of area.

Objectives
- to find the area of rectangles by counting square units and by applying the formula $A = l \times w$
- to explore what happens to the area of a rectangle when one side is doubled
- to explore what happens to the area of a rectangle when both sides are doubled and tripled
- to predict what happens when the dimensions of a rectangle are multiplied by any number

Materials
- graph paper
- "Blowing Up Rectangles" (one per student, pages 20–21)
- calculators (one per group)

Introduction
Using an overhead projector, draw a three-unit by six-unit rectangle on graph paper. Review how to find the length and width of the rectangle. Review how to find the area of the rectangle by counting the square units within the rectangle, and by multiplying the length by the width.

Pose the question "What will happen to the area if I double the length of this rectangle?" Solicit predictions from the class. Demonstrate on the overhead projector what happens when you double only the length of the rectangle. Find the area by counting the square units within the new rectangle and using the formula $A = l \times w$. Repeat this procedure for width.

Enlarging Rectangles
Group students in pairs and distribute "Blowing Up Rectangles." Although they work in pairs, students should keep their own record of their work. If some pairs of students finish early, encourage them to enlarge more rectangles.

Discussing Results
When students have finished the explorations, discuss the results with the whole class. Encourage students to explain their answers to the "Why does this happen?" sections of their worksheets. Generate a class chart summarizing what happens to the area of a rectangle when both sides are multiplied by 2, 3, 4, 5, and other larger numbers. The rectangle used in the example should be small to keep the model manageable. (For example: the original rectangle is 2×3, the original area is 6.)

Multiply Sides By	New Dimensions	New Area (square units)	New Area ÷ Original Area
2	4×6	24	$24 \div 6 = 4$
3	6×9	54	$54 \div 6 = 9$
4	8×12	96	$96 \div 6 = 16$
5	10×15	150	$150 \div 6 = 25$
6	12×18	216	$216 \div 6 = 36$
7	14×21	294	$294 \div 6 = 49$

Conclude by reinforcing that when both sides of a rectangle are multiplied by the same number, the area is increased by the square of that number.

Blowing Up Rectangles

Draw a rectangle on the graph paper, then blow up, or enlarge, the rectangle by multiplying both the length and the width by two. Record the enlarged measurements and the new area. The first rectangle has been enlarged for you. Enlarge the second rectangle, and then create your own rectangles for the last two rows.

Original Rectangle			New Rectangle		
Length	Width	Area	Length × 2	Width × 2	New Area
3	2	6	$3 \times 2 = 6$	$2 \times 2 = 4$	$4 \times 6 = 24$
4	3	12	_____	_____	_____
—	—	—	_____	_____	_____
—	—	—	_____	_____	_____

What is the relationship between the area of original rectangles and the area of the new rectangles?

Why does this happen?

Multiply each dimension of the original rectangles by three. Keep a record of your work.

What is the relationship between the area of the original rectangles and the area of the new rectangles?

Why does this happen?

If you multiplied each dimension by four, how much larger than the original area would the area of the new rectangle be?

Try it with one of the original rectangles to find out.
What general rule applies to enlarging a rectangle if you multiply both dimensions by the same number?

The Box Kite

The box kite was invented by Lawrence Hargrave in the late 1800s. Hargrave was born in England on January 29, 1850, and moved in 1866 to New South Wales, Australia. His father was a judge in the supreme court system and wanted Lawrence to have a career in law. Instead, Lawrence chose to work in science and engineering. At seventeen, he took a job with the Australian Steam and Navigation Company. After working for five years and gaining experience in navigation and engineering, he joined an expedition to explore uncharted lands in the interior of New Guinea. After this adventure, he settled down in Sydney, New South Wales.

In 1878 Hargrave took a position at the Sydney Observatory. There he pursued his lifelong interests. He spent years experimenting with kites, hoping to develop manned flight. In 1893, as a result of his experiments, he invented the box kite. In one experiment, a string of four kites lifted him into the air over the ocean, then dropped him into the water. His box kite was quickly accepted for use in weather observation throughout the world. Hargrave also developed a number of different cellular kites. He never patented his inventions because he felt that they should be used freely for the betterment of mankind. The Wright brothers were influenced by Hargrave's box kite design when they developed their gliders and airplanes.

In the early 1900s, the box kite replaced the Eddy bow kite as the kite used by the U.S. Weather Observatory at Blue Hills, Massachusetts. Box kites were used for weather and atmospheric research until airplanes became popular. Because the flying kites presented a hazard to airplanes, they were replaced by helium balloons. Kites are still used for weather observation in unpopulated areas where they pose little danger to aircraft.

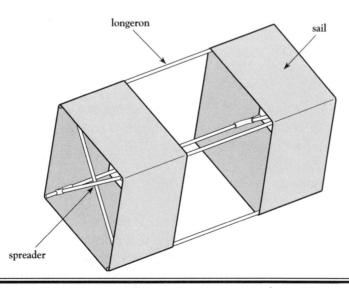

Flat-Style Box Kite Lesson Plan

Objectives

- to find the side of a square
- to find the diagonal of a square
- to develop measuring skills
- to create a rectangular prism
- to improve spatial perception
- to use fractions and proportions to create a pattern

Materials

- plastic trash bags, paper, or fabric for sails
- $\frac{3}{16}$" or $\frac{1}{8}$" dowels—four 48" dowels per kite (have extra dowels on hand in case of breakage)
- one foot of $\frac{3}{16}$" or $\frac{1}{8}$" ID (inner diameter) tubing per kite (extra may be needed)
- tape
- string for bridles
- kite string
- copies of "Directions for Making a Flat-Style Box Kite" (one per student, pages 27–30)
- copies of "The Box Kite" (page 23, optional)
- copies of "Finding the Diagonal of a Square" (pages 38–39, optional)

Equipment

- yardsticks
- scissors
- newsprint for making a pattern (optional)
- permanent markers for decoration (optional)
- needles with large eyes for stringing bridles
- goggles (one pair for each student to wear while their group is connecting spreaders to longerons)

Introduction

Discuss with the whole class the history of the box kite, Lawrence Hargrave, and his drive to develop manned flight. Emphasize the use of kites for observing weather, raising cameras for aerial photographs, and ultimately raising man in tethered flight. The use of the box-kite design in the Wright brothers' experiments should also be pointed out. Distribute "The Box Kite" (optional).

Class Preparation

The class may need to review the concepts of perimeter of a square, diagonal of a square, symmetry, and the meaning of a 90° angle (square corner). The activity "Finding the Diagonal of a Square," prepares students for this lesson.

Making the Pattern and Cutting the Sail

Discuss with the class the properties of a rectangular prism. The prism they will make has a square base. Group the students in pairs or groups of three or four. Tell each group they will have enough dowels to make one large or two small kites. Distribute one set of directions to each student. Supply each group with paper for a pattern (optional) and a yardstick. Instruct the groups to work together with the given materials. Each group is responsible for deciding the final size of their kite(s) and the length of the longerons and spreaders. As the groups work, circulate around the room. Each group member should be able to explain how they determined the diagonal of the square. As each group's calculations are completed, check them for accuracy and discuss the calculations with the group members. After they finish planning the kite, allow them to get materials and cut the sail for the kite. If they want to decorate the sail, they should do it now, before they fasten it to the frame.

Making the Frame

Distribute the four dowels and tubing. If a group chooses to make a kite over 25" long, they need $\frac{3}{16}$" diameter dowels; if they choose a smaller size, $\frac{1}{8}$" dowels will work. Be sure students carefully plan and measure before they cut the dowels, or they might wind up with one short longeron. They must cut the longerons before the spreaders. Demonstrate to the whole class how to make a joiner and slip it on the end of the longeron. If the dowel resists sliding through the joiner, dip the end into liquid soap.

Circulate among the groups asking questions that will promote their understanding of the directions.

Putting It All Together

Following the directions, students tape the longerons to the sails, double checking their measurement and being sure that the joiner is at a 90° angle. Slide the spreaders onto the joiners. This stage will take physical cooperation between the members of the groups. For safety, insist that students wear safety goggles during this stage of the assembly. When the frame is completed, one member should tie the spreaders at 90° angles at the center marks. Be sure that the kite is symmetrical.

Groups will reach this stage at different times. The first group may need help. When the members of this group are finished, they will become the experts who can help other groups assemble their kites.

Bridling

To secure the bridle to the kite, place a piece of strapping tape on the point of contact. Thread the bridle string through the needle and sew the end of the bridle through the tape and around the longeron.

Show students the three ways to bridle their kite. For flying in light winds, the most effective way is a single attachment to the leading edge (figure a). A two-legged bridle on the leading edge (figure b), which allows the angle of attack to be changed easily, is also effective in most light winds. When flying in heavier winds, a four-legged bridle (figure c) will expose less surface to the wind.

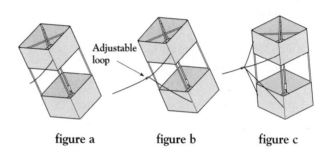

figure a   **figure b**   **figure c**

Streamers attached to the trailing edge may lend stability in flight to a slightly asymmetrical kite.

Sharing

When the kites are finished, the students will want to show and talk about the designs they made. Allow time to discuss the mathematical problems posed in this activity. Ask representatives from different groups to describe to the class how their group found the side of the square and the diagonal of the square. If students discovered more than one way to solve the problem, be sure that each method is discussed.

Student groups will find different methods to solve the math problems; their methods will vary in sophistication. Discuss the strategies for solving the problems within the groups and with the whole class. Methods for finding the diagonal of a square include:
• Use the Pythagorean theorem.
• Multiply the side by 1.41, 1.4, or $\sqrt{2}$.
• Draw the square, then measure the diagonal.

Note

This book includes directions for building two different styles of box kites, flat-style and sheath-style. If, after using this flat-style box kite lesson plan with your students, you decide to build the sheath-style box kite as a follow-up lesson, you need not repeat similar parts of the lesson.

Variations

Some students may want to make minibox kites. Drinking straws may be used as longerons and spreaders with some adaptations. Use tissue paper for the sail and tape the spreaders to the longerons.

Two box kites may be attached at one side to make a rectangular prism. When you bridle this rectangular kite, experiment with a one-point attachment near the top of the center longeron, a two-legged bridle from the center longeron or a four-legged bridle.

Variation in Materials

Fabric may be used to make colorful box kites; use fabric tape for the strapping.

Directions for Making a Flat-Style Box Kite

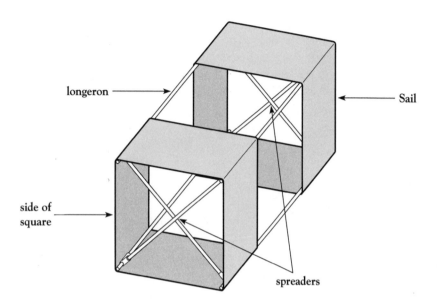

You need these materials:

- sail material—paper or plastic
- $\frac{3}{16}$" or $\frac{1}{8}$" dowel—four dowels per kite
- $\frac{3}{16}$" or $\frac{1}{8}$" ID tubing—one foot for each kite
- tape
- string

Put a check in each box as you complete the step.

Designing the Kite

☐ Decide the size of the kite you will make. Take into account the length of the dowels you have to work with. The ratio of the side of the square base to the length of the kite (side : longeron) is 2 : 5. This means that if you want your kite to be 5" long, the side of the square will be 2". If you want a kite 10" long, the length of the side will be 4".

☐ Decide on the length the longeron of your kite.
The length of the longeron will be _____ .
To find the length of the side of the square base of the kite,
multiply the length of the longeron by $\frac{2}{5}$.
The length of the side of the square base of the kite will be

_____ .

☐ Find the length of the spreaders that keep the kite open. The
spreaders are the length of the diagonal of the square base.
Find the diagonal of the square. Round the diagonal up to the
nearest half inch. How did you find the diagonal? Show your
work here.

The length for each of the four spreaders will be _____ .

☐ Find the total length of the dowels you will need to make
your kite.
The length of the longeron will be _____ inches long.
The length of the spreader will be _____ inches long.
Add the lengths of the longeron and spreader.
You will need four dowels _____ inches long.
If you decide on a kite 25" or less in length, use $\frac{1}{8}$" dowels. If
your kite will be longer, use $\frac{3}{16}$" dowels.

☐ Cut the longerons and spreaders from your dowels.

☐ Mark the center of each spreader.

Making the Sails

☐ Find the dimensions of the sail. The two identical rectangular
sails wrap around either end of the kite. Their measurements
are based on the length of the square base. Find the width of
the sail by multiplying the side of the square by $\frac{2}{3}$.
The width of each rectangular sail is _____ .
Find the length of the sail by multiplying the side of the
square by four. Add one inch for overlap. The length of the
sail is _____ .
The sail is a rectangle _____ long and _____ wide.

☐ Cut two sails the size of this rectangle.

Making the Frame

☐ Make eight joiners from tubing. To make a joiner, cut $1\frac{1}{2}''$ of tubing. Find the middle of this piece and cut halfway through the tubing. Bend the joiner 90° at the cut.

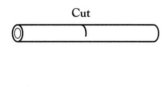

Cut

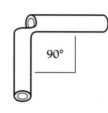

90°

☐ Slip joiners onto the ends of the longerons and slide them down each end a distance of one-third the length of the sail.

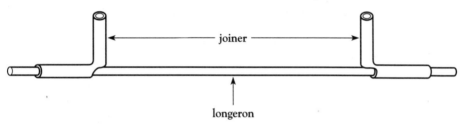

joiner

longeron

Putting It All Together

☐ Spread sails out on a flat surface as shown in the illustration. Place the longerons on the sails making sure that the joiners point up at a 90° angle. Tape the longerons to the sails at the indicated points (square marks). Tape the other end of the sail to the one-inch overlap and the first longeron.

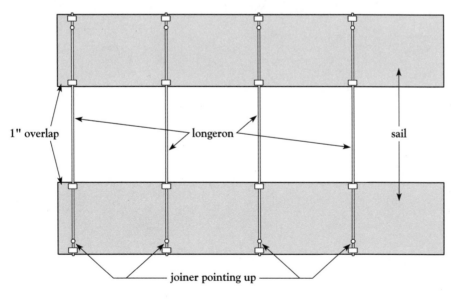

1" overlap   longeron   sail

joiner pointing up

☐ Slide the spreaders into place being careful not to break them.

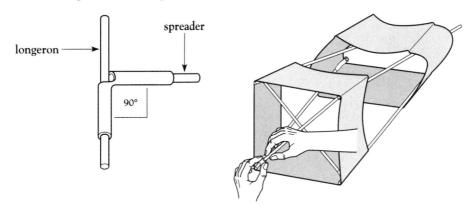

Make any adjustments in the length of the spreaders by snipping off $\frac{1}{4}$" at a time. Tie the spreaders in the middle to maintain a 90° angle.

☐ Bridle the kite with one leg for light winds, two legs for medium wind, or four legs for heavy wind.

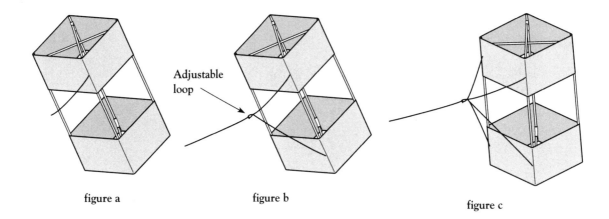

figure a   figure b   figure c

Sheath-Style Box Kite Lesson Plan

Objectives

- to find the dimensions of a square given the perimeter
- to find the diagonal of a square
- to develop measuring skills
- to create a rectangular prism
- to improve spatial perception required to understand diagrams
- to find if the area of a shape is between 25 and 50 square inches

Materials

- tall kitchen trash bags (these measure approximately 24" by 25"–30")
- $\frac{3}{16}$" dowel—four 48" dowels per kite (have extras on hand in case of breakage)
- one foot of $\frac{3}{16}$" ID (inner diameter) tubing per kite (extra may be needed)
- tape (strapping tape is best, but masking tape can be used)
- copies of "Directions for Making a Sheath-Style Box Kite" (one per student, pages 34–36)
- string for bridles
- copies of "The Box Kite" (page 23, optional)
- copies of "Finding the Diagonal of a Square" (page 38, optional)

Equipment

- yardsticks
- sharp scissors or skill knives
- permanent markers for decoration (optional)
- needles with large eyes (for string)
- goggles (one pair for each student to wear while their group is connecting spreaders to longerons)

Introduction

Discuss Lawrence Hargrave and his drive to develop manned flight. Stress the use of kites for observing weather, raising cameras for aerial photographs, and raising man in tethered flight. Point out that the Wright brothers used the box kite design in their experiments. You may want to distribute copies of "The Box Kite."

Class Preparation

The class needs to know the concepts of perimeter of a square, diagonal of a square, symmetry, and 90° angle (square corner). Complete the activity "Finding the Diagonal of a Square" before building the kite. Break the class into groups of three or four.

Making the Frame

Open a bag and, with a student volunteer, stick your arms into it, forming a rough rectangular prism to demonstrate how the bag will become the outside covering of the kite.

Discuss with the class the properties of a rectangular prism—the prism used to make the box kite will have a square base. Distribute one set of directions to each student and one trash bag and yardstick to each group. Instruct the groups to work together to find the length of the longerons and spreaders. As the groups work, circulate around the room asking questions to assess their understanding. Every group member should be able to explain how their group found the dimensions of the square. As each group's calculations are completed and checked, distribute the four dowels needed for the project. Each dowel will make one longeron and one spreader. Be sure students cut the longerons first, or there may not be enough dowels.

Demonstrate to the whole class how to make a joiner and slip it on the end of the longerons. If the dowels resist sliding through the joiner, dip the ends of it into liquid soap. As each group finishes cutting the dowels, distribute 12" of tubing to each group. The groups should now be able to follow the directions to complete the frame. Circulate among the groups and ask questions that will help them understand the directions.

Making the Sheath

Instruct the whole class to make vents for their kites. The shape of the vent lends individuality to the kites. Explain that the vents should be compact; squares, circles, stars, and triangles all make appropriate vents, but long rectangles do not. As you circulate among the groups, discuss their vents with them individually. Before cutting out the vent, the group should be able to demonstrate to you that the area of the vent is between 25 and 50 square inches. If students want to decorate their kites, they should do it before the sheath is put on the frame.

Putting It All Together

This stage will take physical cooperation between the members of the groups. For safety, insist that students wear safety goggles during this stage of the assembly. When the frame is opened up, one member should tape the spreaders at the center marks. Be sure that the frame is symmetrical.

Groups will reach this stage at different times. The first group may need help. When the members of this group are finished, they will become the experts who can help other groups assemble their kites.

Bridling

Show students how to secure the bridle to the kite. Place a piece of strapping tape on the point of contact. Thread the bridle string through a needle and sew the end of the bridle through the tape and around the longeron.

There are three ways to bridle this kite. In light winds, the most effective way is a single attachment to the leading edge (figure a). A two-legged bridle on the leading edge (figure b), which allows the angle of attack to be changed easily, is also effective in most light winds. When flying in heavier winds, a four-legged bridle (figure c) will expose less surface to the wind. Streamers may be attached to the trailing edge to lend stability to a slightly asymmetrical kite.

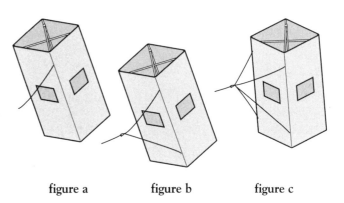

figure a   figure b   figure c

Sharing

When the kites are finished, the students will want to share their designs. Be sure to reserve time to discuss the mathematical problems posed in this activity. Ask representatives from different groups to describe how their group found the side of the square and the diagonal of the square. If students found more than one way to solve the problem, be sure that each method is discussed. Each group should be able to prove to the class that their vent is between 25 and 50 square inches.

Notes

Groups will use different methods to solve the math problems. These will vary in sophistication. Methods for determining the side of the square include:

- Divide the width of the bag by two.
- Double the width to get the perimeter of the box, and divide the perimeter by four.
- Fold the bag in fourths, then measure it.

Methods for finding the diagonal of a square include:

- Use the Pythagorean theorem.
- Multiply the side by 1.41, 1.4, or $\sqrt{2}$.
- Draw the square, and then measure the diagonal.

Methods for proving that the area of a figure is between 25 and 50 square inches include:

- Make a polygon or circle and use the standard formulas.
- Make two figures, one with an area of 25 square inches and one with an area of 50 square inches; cut out the vent shape and physically compare it to the two figures, to prove that it fits between these two standards.

Directions for Making a Sheath-Style Box Kite

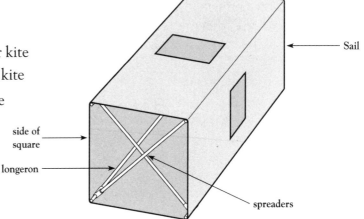

Sail

side of square

longeron

spreaders

You need these materials:

- tall kitchen trash bags—one per kite
- $\frac{3}{16}$" dowel—four 48" dowels per kite
- $\frac{3}{16}$" ID tubing—one foot per kite
- tape
- string

Put a check in each box as you complete the step.

Making the Frame

☐ The trash bag will form a sheath for the outside of the kite. Lay the bag flat. Measure its length and subtract $\frac{1}{4}$". This is the length of the longerons. Write the measurement here.

_____

☐ Measure the width of the bag. The opening of the bag forms the square base of the box kite. Find the length of the side of the square. Explain how you found the side of the square. Show your work.

☐ Find the length of the diagonal of the square to the nearest half inch. Explain how you found the diagonal of the square.

This is the length of the four spreaders that will keep the kite open. Write the measurement here. _____

☐ Cut the longerons and spreaders from your $\frac{3}{16}$" dowels. Be sure to cut the longerons first.

- [ ] Make eight joiners from $\frac{3}{16}$" ID tubing. To make a joiner, cut a $1\frac{1}{2}$" length of tubing. Find the middle of this piece and cut halfway through the tubing. Bend the joiner 90° at the cut.

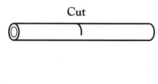 

- [ ] Slide joiners 3" down on each end of the longerons.

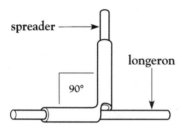

- [ ] Join two spreaders and two longerons to form a rectangle. Form a second rectangle with the remaining two spreaders and longerons. Be sure that the joints are at 90° angles.

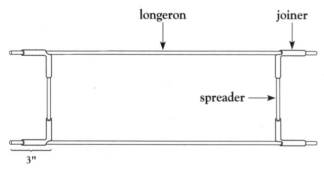

- [ ] Find and mark the center of each spreader.

Making the Sheath

- [ ] Decide what your vent will look like. The vent may be any shape that has an area between 25 and 50 square inches. Long, thin shapes do not work as well as compact shapes such as squares and circles. Make a pattern of the vent.

- [ ] Fold the bag into fourths lengthwise. Center the vent pattern on the folded bag and trace. Cut out the vent through all four layers.

- [ ] Slit the bottom of the bag open.

Putting It All Together

This takes at least four hands!

☐ Cross the spreaders at the center marks to form the frame. Collapse the frame so it can slide easily into the bag. Open the sheath.

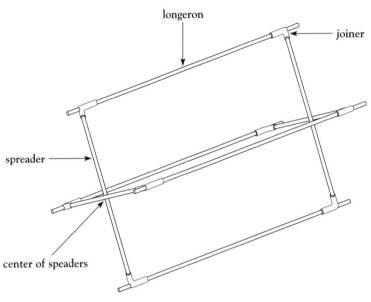

Frame

☐ Slide the frame into the sheath and open it to form a square base. The spreaders will bow slightly out. One person holds the spreaders while the other tapes them at 90° angles.

☐ Work the bag over the frame until the kite is as symmetrical as possible. Tie the spreaders together. Secure the sheath by taping over the ends of the longerons.

Attaching the Bridle

☐ Attach the bridle as shown.

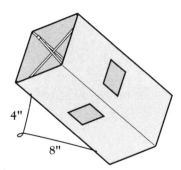

Finding the Diagonal of a Square Lesson Plan

There are several ways to find the diagonal of a square. In this exploration, students will discover that there is a constant ratio of 1 to approximately 1.4 between the length of the side and diagonal of a square.

Objectives

- to solve a problem by making models, developing a systematic list, and applying observations to similar situations
- to develop an understanding of the properties of a square
- to measure correctly to the nearest millimeter
- to discover the relationship between the length of the side and diagonal of a square
- to develop and apply a rule to find the diagonal of a square given the length of the side

Materials

- centimeter graph paper—one sheet for each group (page 40)
- metric ruler that measures to the nearest millimeter—one for each group
- copies of "Finding the Diagonal of a Square" (pages 38–39)—one for each student
- calculator—one for each group

Introduction

Review the properties of a square with the class, including the terms right angle, quadrilateral, side, and diagonal. Review measuring a line to the nearest tenth of a centimeter (millimeter). Discuss what to do when the length of the object you are measuring falls between lines of measure. Students can work in pairs or small groups, but individual students need their own copies of the worksheet so they can keep their own record of their work.

Answers

Numbers in the middle column may differ by one or two millimeters depending on the measuring instrument and graph paper.

Side of Square	Diagonal of Square	Diagonal ÷ Side
2	2.8	1.4
4	5.6 (5.7)	1.4
5	7.1	1.4
7	9.9	1.4
10	14.1	1.4
15	21.2	1.4

A square with a side of 8 cm has a diagonal of 11.2 cm.

Extensions

Ask students to use the Pythagorean theorem to find the diagonal of a square that has a side one unit long. They will discover that the diagonal of a one-unit square is the square root of two, an irrational number. The unending, nonrepeating decimal that approximates the square root of two begins 1.414213 . . . .

Finding the Diagonal of a Square

Is there a consistent relationship between the diagonal of a square and its side? Find the answer by investigating.

Make squares with the following sides on centimeter graph paper.

2   4   5   7   10   15

Measure the diagonal of each square to the nearest tenth of a centimeter. Write the measurement in the proper space on the chart.

Divide the diagonal by the side, and fill in the last column of the chart.

Side of Square	Diagonal of Square	Diagonal ÷ Side (to the nearest millimeter)
2		
4		
5		
7		
10		
15		

© Dale Seymour Publications

Building Kites

Look carefully at the results in the last column. Can you see a pattern? If so what is it? Write your observations here.

Using your observation, how could you find the diagonal of a square that has a side 8 cm long? Show your calculations.

On the back of this page, draw a square with a side of 8 cm and measure the diagonal. Were your calculations correct? _____

Draw a few more squares of various sizes, and find their diagonals.

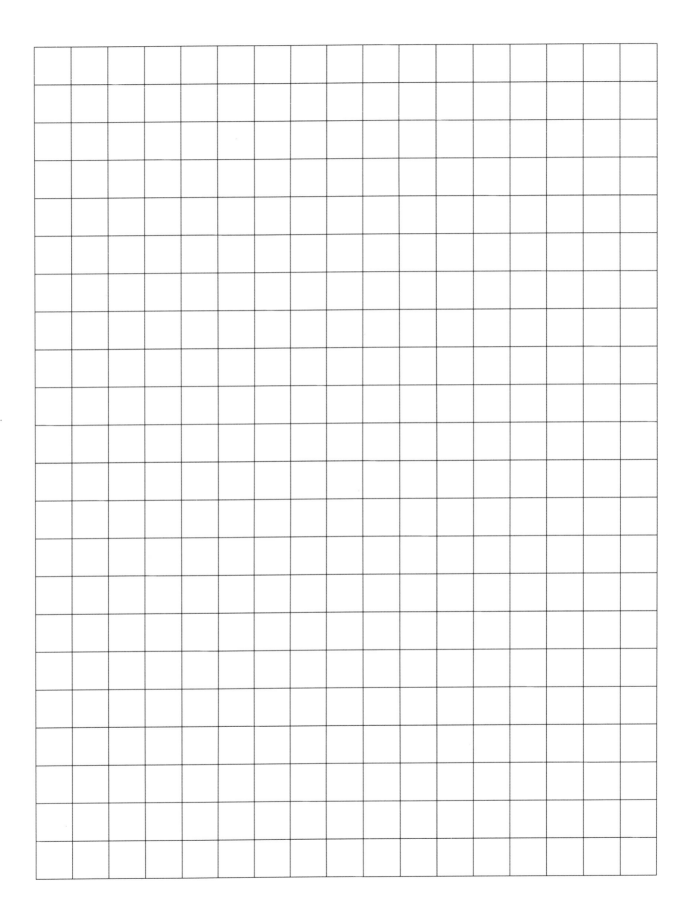

The Tetrahedral Kite

The tetrahedral kite was developed by the man best known as the inventor of the telephone—Alexander Graham Bell. Few people realize that he was also a pioneer in manned flight. Bell was born in Edinburgh, Scotland in 1847, and moved to Canada when he was in his early twenties. He and his family were interested in the science of speech and sound. After he invented the telephone, he moved to Washington, D.C., where he worked with the deaf and helped to develop the gramophone. He became a United States citizen, but in 1893 he moved back to Nova Scotia.

Bell was fascinated with the prospect of manned flight. Like the Wright brothers, he began experimenting with Hargrave's box kite. After making many variations on the box kite, he changed his focus to work with tetrahedrons. A regular tetrahedron has four faces, each of which is an equilateral triangle. Bell's tetrahedral kites contained many tetrahedrons, or tetrahedral cells. Two of the four faces of each cell were covered with silk and the remaining two faces were left open. These tetrahedral cells can be combined in many ways, making a variety of kites possible from the basic tetrahedral unit.

On December 6, 1907, Bell launched his first manned kite named the *Cygnet*. The *Cygnet* was made of 3,393 cells and weighed 208 pounds. Bell also designed it to float. U.S. Army Lieutenant Thomas E. Selfridge volunteered to test the *Cygnet*, and rode in the kite's center. The kite was pulled by a steamer over Baddeck Bay, Nova Scotia. It rose 168 feet in the air and flew for seven minutes. The *Cygnet* landed safely on the water, but the boat crew did not let go of the towrope quickly enough, and the kite was dragged through the water and ruined. Selfridge ended his test flight wet but safe. Less than a year later Selfridge was a passenger on Orville Wright's third passenger-carrying flight. The plane crashed and Selfridge died.

Bell later built *Cygnet II*, which had an engine, but could not fly. Many of Bell's kites are still on display in the Alexander Graham Bell Museum in Baddeck, Nova Scotia.

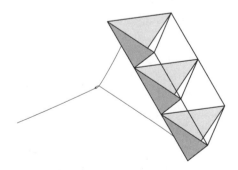

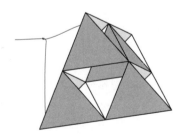

Tetrahedral Kite Lesson Plan

The tetrahedral kite is exciting to build. It flies well, is colorful, and makes a stunning classroom display. By adding successive layers of cells, students can build tetrahedral kites that reach from the floor to the ceiling. The number-theory lesson "Square and Triangular Numbers" applies to the number of tetrahedral cells in each layer of the tetrahedral kite and may be used before or at the conclusion of this unit.

Objectives
- to develop an understanding of geometric terms: tetrahedron, face, pyramid, base, vertex, edge
- to create a tetrahedron
- to find a pattern of numbers from a sequence
- to visualize a series of tetrahedrons in three dimensions

Materials
- drinking straws—at least 120 per group
- tissue paper or light plastic trash bags
- glue sticks or tape
- string
- $\frac{1}{8}$" dowel to pass through the leading edge (one per kite)
- heavy paper for pattern
- copies of "Directions for Making a Tetrahedral Kite" (one per student, pages 45–46)
- copies of "The Tetrahedral Kite" (page 41, optional)
- copies of "Square and Triangular Numbers" (pages 49–51, optional)

Equipment
- large-eyed needles (at least two per group)
- scissors

Introduction

Distribute sets of six straws to pairs of students and ask them to make four equilateral triangles from the six straws without cutting the straws. To find the solution, students must think in three dimensions. First they form one triangle on the desk with three straws, and then hold the other three straws in the air over the center of the first triangle to form three edges that meet at the apex and connect to the three vertices of the triangle on the desk. If students do not find the solution after a few minutes, ask questions that will lead them to a solution.

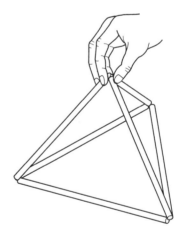

Using a model of a tetrahedron, talk about the word parts: *tetra* (four) and *hedron* (face). A *tetrahedron* is a three-dimensional figure with four faces. It can also be described as a pyramid with four sides or a triangular pyramid. Using the model, develop the other vocabulary words—equilateral, face, edge, vertex—and reinforce these words during this activity.

Discuss Alexander Graham Bell's fascination with kites, his interest in manned flight, and his extensive work with tetrahedral kites.

Class Preparation

As the students build these kites, they will find that each layer is made from a successive triangular number of cells. (A triangular number of objects—such as 3, 6, or 10—can be formed into a triangle.) The worksheet "Square and Triangular Numbers" may be presented to the class before, after, or during this activity.

Making the Tetrahedrons

Divide the class into groups of four or five for this activity. Pass out "Directions for Making a Tetrahedral Kite." Demonstrate to the whole class how to follow the directions to make the frame of a tetrahedron. To get the string through the straws, thread the string into a needle and drop the needle through the straw. Before presenting this activity, check to be sure the threaded needle will pass through the straws you are using. Students often have difficulty tying knots that will not slip. The students in each group may set up divisions of labor (knot tier, straw threader, gluer) to capitalize on the individual skills of group members.

Each group must decide how many layers of cells they want their kite to have, and then figure out how many one-unit tetrahedrons they will have to construct. Ask the groups to consider what they want from their kite. Kites containing five or more layers will be too large to fit through the classroom door; they are impressive but purely decorative. Kites of four layers fly well in a moderate breeze, while kites of two or three layers fly best in a mild breeze.

Making the Pattern and Covering the Frames

Once they have a few frames made, each group should make a pattern to use when cutting out the covering. The covering is cut from tissue paper or plastic, placed over two sides of the tetrahedron, and glued or taped in place. Glue sticks should be used to attach tissue paper to frame, and tape should be used for plastic covers.

Assembling

When a group has all the units it needs, the students should place the bottom layer on the table with all the covered sides facing the front, and tie the corners at the base of each unit together. Next the students balance the vertices of the bases of the next layer on the lower tetrahedrons, and tie them together. They continue to build the kite.

Reinforcing the Leading Edge

When the kite is completed, run a dowel down the inside of the straws in the leading edge. Place tape over the ends of the top and bottom straws to keep the dowel from slipping out.

Bridling

Refer to the diagram in "Directions for Making a Tetrahedral Kite" for the position of the bridle. Reinforce the attachment points with tape. Thread a needle with kite string and pierce the tape. Tie the bridle securely.

Notes

The material used for covering the kite depends on the intended use. Tissue paper is bright and colorful: students can make impressive kites by combining the many available colors. Kites made from tissue paper fly well, but are easily torn. If the grass is wet or the kite lands in a puddle, the paper will disintegrate.

Light plastic is sturdier than tissue paper, although not as attractive. Plastic stands up better under difficult flying conditions and is not affected by dampness. Clear plastic makes an interesting kite covering because the frame can be seen through it.

Variations

Students can make larger tetrahedral units using dowels for the frame and plastic trash bags as the covering. They will need to decide how to attach the three dowels at each vertex. Four of these larger dowel-framed units (18" on a side) can be made into a two-layered kite with a 36" edge that flies well in moderate winds. (Use gloves for flying this kite to avoid cuts or rope burns.)

Usually, a four-layer kite is made of layers of ten, six, three, and one units. Students may notice that in a two-layered kite made of four units, an upside-down unit is missing from the center. This observation may lead them to design a four-layer kite from 4 four-unit kites, with a total of 16 units. This kite is lighter than the standard four-layer kite, and flies equally well.

Directions for Making a Tetrahedral Kite

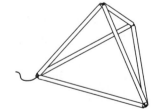

You need these materials:

- six straws per cell
- string
- covering (tissue paper or plastic trash bags)
- glue sticks or tape
- $\frac{1}{8}$" dowel

Put a check in each box as you complete the step.

Building One Cell

A tetrahedron is a triangular pyramid with four faces; each face is an equilateral triangle. You will make the six edges of the tetrahedron out of straws.

☐ Make a triangle out of three straws by running string through them and tying the string in a solid knot.

☐ Add two more straws to one side of the triangle and tie them so you have two triangles with a common side. It should look like this.

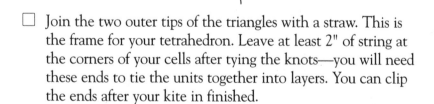

☐ Join the two outer tips of the triangles with a straw. This is the frame for your tetrahedron. Leave at least 2" of string at the corners of your cells after tying the knots—you will need these ends to tie the units together into layers. You can clip the ends after your kite in finished.

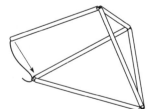

☐ Make a pattern of two joined triangles and a margin of about one inch. Cut the covering the size of this pattern, and glue or tape it to two of the tetrahedron's faces. The leading edge of the kite is where the two covered faces meet. Fly it as a single kite, or join more tetrahedrons to make a larger kite.

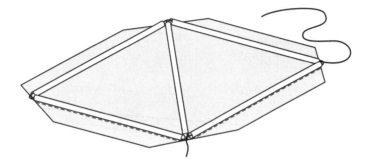

Building Larger Kites

Larger kites may be made by joining tetrahedrons in layers. The numbers of tetrahedrons in successive layers form an interesting mathematical pattern.

- The top layer has one tetrahedron, so a single-layer kite has one tetrahedron.
- The second layer has three tetrahedrons, so a two-layer kite has four tetrahedrons.
- The third layer has six tetrahedrons, so a three-layer kite has ten tetrahedrons.

If you discover the number pattern, you will be able to figure out how many tetrahedrons you need for any size kite. Just make sure you can get the finished kite through the door to fly it!

☐ Run a $\frac{1}{8}$" dowel down the inside of the straws in the leading edge to strengthen it; then bridle the kite as shown.

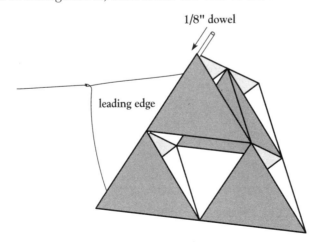

1/8" dowel

leading edge

Square and Triangular Numbers Lesson Plan

Your students may be interested in learning about Pythagoras, a Greek philosopher and mathematician who lived in the sixth century B.C. He studied many aspects of mathematics including square and triangular numbers. His name is familiar; it is the name of the theorem that relates the lengths of the sides of right triangles.

Most middle-school students are already familiar with square numbers, but are often unaware of triangular numbers. This series of open-ended explorations of number patterns will help students see the relationship between a sequence of triangular numbers and the structure of the tetrahedral kite. The successive layers of a tetrahedral kite are made up of triangular numbers. You can determine how many small tetrahedrons make up a larger tetrahedral kite by adding the triangular numbers in each layer.

Objectives

- to review the concept of square numbers
- to discover a pattern in the sequence of triangular numbers
- to describe in words a number pattern
- to find a relationship between numbers
- to find the nth number in a series
- to derive an algebraic formula from a number pattern
- to explore triangular and square numbers and the relationship between them

Materials

- copies of "Square and Triangular Numbers" (one per student, pages 49–51)
- calculators (one per group)
- circular chips or pennies

Introduction

Using circular chips or pennies on an overhead projector, form square arrays to demonstrate square numbers. Ask class members to predict the next number in the series as you build squares.

$$1, 4, 9, 16, \ldots$$

Square numbers are obtained by multiplying a number by itself. For example, $3 \times 3 = 9$ and $12 \times 12 = 144$.

Introduce triangular numbers in the same manner. Build the first four triangular numbers—1, 3, 6, and 10—with the class. Ask the class to think about this question: "Is there a way to predict the next triangular number in a sequence?"

Break the class into pairs or groups of four and distribute the worksheets. Circulate to ask appropriate questions as they work. As students approach question 8, use the coins or circular chips to demonstrate to the whole class, or to selected groups, how to break the squares into two triangular numbers as illustrated on the worksheet.

Most students will be able to complete these explorations with the aid of a calculator. In a heterogeneous class, some advanced students may be able to take this activity as far as discovering the algebraic formula to find the nth triangular number in the series: nth Δ number $= \left(\frac{1}{2}n + \frac{1}{2}\right)n$.

Answers

	1st	2d	3d	4th	5th	6th	7th	8th	9th	10th
Triangular numbers	1	3	6	10	15	21	28	36	45	55

1. Answers will vary. Example: Starting with zero, add consecutive numbers to the preceding triangular number. $1 + 2 = 3$, then $3 + 3 = 6$, then $6 + 4 = 10$, etc.
2. Answers will vary. Example: To find the fourth triangular number, add $1 + 2 + 3 + 4 = 10$.
3. Example: Yes. $1 + 2 + 3 + 4 + 5 + 6 + 7 = 28$.
4. Answers will vary.
5. 5050.
6. Answers will vary. Some students will add all the numbers from 1 to 100. A more sophisticated answer would be to list all numbers from 1 to 100 with the 50 pairs marked that add up to 101. Then multiply the number of pairs by the sum of each pair: $50 \times 101 = 5050$.

$$1, 2, 3, 4, \ldots 97, 98, 99, 100$$

with brackets showing 101, 101, 101, 101

50 pairs of $101 = 5050$

Advanced students may explore to find that the following formula holds true for *even* triangular numbers:

The sixth triangular number is 21.

$21 = 3 \times 7 \quad 3 = \frac{1}{2}(6)$ and $7 = 6 + 1$

thus nth triangular number $= \frac{1}{2}n(n + 1)$

After exploring with *odd* triangular numbers, students may discover the following formula

The seventh triangular number is 28

28 is $7 \times 4 \quad 4 = 3\frac{1}{2} + \frac{1}{2}$

nth $\triangle$ number is $(\frac{1}{2}n + \frac{1}{2})n$

Further exploration will lead the student to discover that the formula for *odd* numbers holds true for *even* numbers as well.

7. $45 + 55 = 100$. The ninth triangular number plus the tenth triangular number equals the tenth square number.
8. Possible answer: Look at the chart on the worksheet.
9. 24th plus 25th $\triangle$ numbers = 25th $\square$ number ($300 + 325 = 625$).

Square and Triangular Numbers

Square numbers are numbers that can be arranged in a square.
They form a pattern.

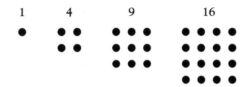

A square number is obtained by multiplying a number by itself.
For example, $3 \times 3 = 9$ and $12 \times 12 = 144$.

There are also numbers that can be arranged in a triangle.
These triangular numbers also form a pattern.

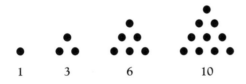

Is there a way to predict the next triangular number in a
sequence?

Fill in the missing triangular numbers.

Triangular Numbers	1st	2d	3d	4th	5th	6th	7th	8th	9th	10th
	1	3	6	10						

1. Describe the pattern you used to find the triangular numbers.

2. Study the relationship between the order of the triangular
    number and the triangular number itself. For example, can
    you find a relationship between the fourth number, 10, and
    the number four?

3. Does this same relationship exist between 7 and the 7th
    triangular number?

4. Describe the relationship you have discovered.

5. What is the 100th triangular number?

6. Describe how you found it.

The layers of a tetrahedral kite are made up of triangular numbers
of tetrahedrons. You will be able to determine how many small
tetrahedrons make up a larger tetrahedral kite by adding the
triangular numbers in each layer. For example, to find the number
of smaller tetrahedrons in a four-layered tetrahedral kite, add the
first four triangular numbers: 1 + 3 + 6 + 10 = 20; thus the four-
layered kite is made of 20 tetrahedrons.

© Dale Seymour Publications

It is interesting to note that every square number is the sum of two consecutive triangular numbers. For example, using the symbols □ and Δ for square and triangular:

1st Δ number + 2d Δ number = 2d □ number, thus 1 + 3 = 4

2d Δ number + 3d Δ number = 3d □ number, thus 3 + 6 = 9

3d Δ number + 4th Δ number = 4th □ number, thus 6 + 10 = 16

7. Which two consecutive triangular numbers can be added together to make a sum of 100?

8. How did you find them?

9. Which two consecutive triangular numbers can be added together to make a sum of 25^2?

Flying Kites

People fly kites not only for entertainment but also in contests and religious ceremonies. For centuries, people in Indonesia, India, Thailand, Korea, Japan, and China have held kite-fighting contests. Fighting kites are small, tailless, and very well balanced and maneuverable. A portion of the flying line is covered with pieces of broken glass or pottery so it will be able to cut another kite's line. Flying these kites takes much practice and skill. Often their construction and design is a family secret, passed down through the generations. There are many forms of fighting-kite contests, but they all involve trying to cut a rival's string and set his kite free to drift in the wind.

In Asia and Polynesia, people believed that an airborne kite attracted the attention of the spirits. Often kites were equipped with wind harps or bamboo whistles so that they would be heard as well as seen by the spirits, and the prayers of the kite fliers would be heard.

In China, ritual kite flying was a part of the seventh birthday celebration of the oldest boy. The father built a kite and collected as much string as he could. The kite was flown, and when it was as far away as possible, the string was cut to let the kite take the boy's bad luck away with it. Because of their religious significance, kites were outlawed by the Communist government in China for many years. The Chinese government today has relaxed the ban and is allowing the Chinese to fly kites once again.

In Korea, a kite celebration takes place during the first 15 days of the year. Parents write on kites the names and birthdays of children they wish to protect from evil spirits. When the kites are flown and released, the spirits are directed away from the children.

Today kite flying is a hobby for thousands of children and adults throughout the world. Local, national, and international kite festivals draw thousands of participants and spectators. Stunt kites—kites made with two lines for greater control and with so much pull that it takes a team of adults to fly them—are gaining popularity. Trains of kites, some containing more than 2,000 kites, are among the many kite variations flown today.

How to Fly a Kite
Lesson Plan

Objectives
- to launch and fly kites
- to repair or adjust kites to fly better

Materials
- kites
- repair kit—tape, extra string, extra tail material, extra spars, and a pair of scissors
- copies of "Flying Kites" (page 53, optional)
- copies of "How to Fly a Kite" (page 55)
- copies of "Safety Rules" (page 56)

Introduction

As your class prepares to fly their kites, share with them some information about flying kites. You may give your students copies of "Flying Kites."

The day before flying, distribute and discuss "How to Fly a Kite" and "Safety Rules." If students are expected to bring in their own kite string, stress that neither fish line nor wire can be used.

Check the weather forecast and choose a day with a light breeze. Most kites fly best with steady rather than turbulent or gusty winds. On the kite-flying day, find an adult volunteer or staff member to join you.

Kite Flying

Students should fly their kites with the group that constructed the kite. You can limit the number of kites in the air at one time by having students take turns with their partners. This reduces the possibility of tangled lines.

Launching the kite is a team effort. It takes two people, a launcher and a flier. The launcher faces the wind and holds the kite over his or her head. The flier faces the launcher, lets out 40 to 50 feet of line, and then signals to the launcher to let go as the flier tugs on the line. As the kite climbs, the flier alternately lets out line and tugs on the string. Many students prefer to run with kites. As students mature, they enjoy learning how to play out the line.

Troubleshooting

Problems may appear when students fly their creations. Encourage any students who have difficulty flying their kites to carefully observe their classmates' successful kites. Ask students about the symmetry of their kites, especially in relation to the weight of the tails. Most flying problems are the result of too much weight on one side and can be solved by adding or snipping tails. Problems with the bridle are also common. Bring the directions for bridling the kite to the field with you. Changing the angle of attack is often helpful. Encourage students to observe the kites in the air and to make bridle adjustments based upon their observations.

It takes a few minutes to reel in a kite, so be sure to give students plenty of warning before you have to leave.

How to Fly a Kite

First check the wind. Observe which way the wind is blowing, how strong it is, and how steady it is. Although many people think that a strong wind is preferable for kite flying, most kites fly better in a gentle wind. Strong winds can tear kites and break spars. If the wind is gusty, the kite may not stay up because of unsteady wind direction and strength.

To launch a kite, stand with your back to the wind. For best results, use a partner as your launcher. The launcher faces the wind and holds the kite over his or her head. You let out 40 to 50 feet of line. (If there is little wind, let out 100 or more feet.) When you are ready, signal the launcher to let go of the kite as you tug on the line. As the kite climbs, let out line. Alternately tugging and letting out line will help your kite to climb.

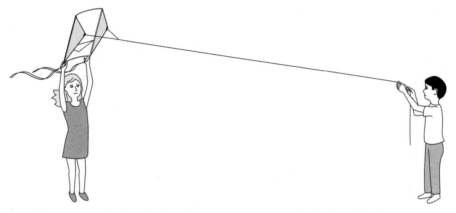

Many people think that the proper way to launch a kite is to run. It takes a lot of concentration to run and launch a kite at the same time. When you are running, you change direction, which puts your kite in a crosswind. The best way to fly a kite is to stand and play out line.

When it is time to start bringing your kite in, reel it in slowly. If the kite begins to fall, relax the line so that it will right itself. When the kite is righted again, you can begin to reel in again, or let it drift to the ground.

If your kite string gets caught on the string of another kite, don't pull! Walk slowly toward the other kite flyer. The person with the lower string should walk under the upper string. This procedure will save both your kites and the string.

Safety Rules

To make sure that your kite-flying experience is a good one, follow these rules.

- Fly your kite in flat, open spaces.

- Don't fly your kite over people. A falling kite is dangerous.

- Stay away from power lines. If your kite does land on a power line, LEAVE IT THERE. Notify the local utility company. DO NOT TRY TO GET IT DOWN YOURSELF! Don't even tug on the string.

- Do not fly a kite in stormy or rainy weather. People have been killed trying to repeat Benjamin Franklin's experiment.

- Wear gloves when flying a strong-pulling kite. Kite string can cut.

- Don't fly near airfields or in airplane traffic patterns. Kites have caused airplane crashes.

- Don't use wire or fish line to fly your kite, it will not break if people get tangled in the line.

- Be careful of birds when you fly your kite. Kite strings can cut their wings.

© Dale Seymour Publications

How High Is the Kite?
Lesson Plan

Students can determine how high a kite is flying using a simple, student-made model of an astrolabe and an estimate of the ground distance between the kite flier and a point directly under the kite.

Objectives

- to review the number of degrees in a circle and right angle
- to use an astrolabe
- to estimate a distance by counting off paces
- to review the parts of the right triangle
- to introduce the use of the tangent function to find a length
- to use the astrolabe and the tangent function to find the height of a kite

Materials

- kite string or heavy thread (12" per student)
- weight—nut, washer, or heavy paper clip (one per student)
- drinking straw (one per student)
- oaktag or light cardboard (one 8" by $5\frac{1}{2}$" piece per student)
- copies of "Making an Astrolabe" (one per student, pages 60–61)
- copies of "Finding Your Own Pace" (one per student, page 62)
- copies of "How High Is the Kite?" (one per student, pages 63–64)
- copies of "Tangent Table" (page 65, optional)

Equipment

- yardstick or long tape measure (you may be able to borrow one from the physical education department)
- tape
- glue
- scissors
- calculators (one per group)

Introduction

Ask the class how ancient navigators found their way around the ocean when they were out of sight of land. Listen to the discussion, which will turn to reading the stars with instruments. Tell students that they will make a simple astrolabe—an instrument used in medieval times to determine how many degrees above the horizon a celestial object was. This instrument can also be used to find the approximate height of tall objects such as trees and buildings. The class will use it to find out how high their kites are flying.

If necessary, review the number of degrees in a circle and in a right angle.

Making the Astrolabe

Students should work in pairs following the directions in "Making an Astrolabe." Make an astrolabe ahead of time to use as a model. Distribute the necessary materials and circulate around the room asking questions to help students solve the problems they encounter. It should take 15 minutes for the students to make the astrolabe.

Demonstrate to the class how to look through an astrolabe and to take a reading in the room. Be sure to show the students how to hold the string against the astrolabe when bringing it down from their eye to read the angle. Ask students to stay seated and take a reading by aiming at a designated point where the ceiling meets the wall perhaps in the corner of the room. Appoint one student to record the readings on the board for the class. Ask different students to give their readings. The students will begin to notice that everyone has a different reading. Ask the students why the readings are different. (Each person has to point his or her astrolabe at a different angle because they are different distances from the wall.) Is there a pattern to the readings? (The students closer to the point will have larger angle readings.) Determine another point in the room—perhaps where the back wall meets the ceiling—and take readings again. Ask students to predict which students will have the lowest readings. Confirm the estimates by having students give their readings to the class.

On the overhead projector, draw a cross section of the room with a right triangle whose sides are formed by the distance along the floor from the student's desk to the wall, the distance along the wall from floor to designated point on the ceiling, and the distance between the point where the ceiling and wall intersect and the student's desk. Review the parts of the right angle including the legs, hypotenuse, right angle, and acute angles.

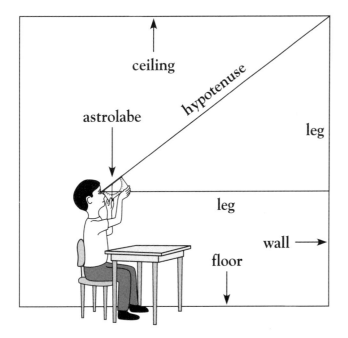

The branch of mathematics called trigonometry is the study of the relationships between the sides and angles of right triangles. Mathematicians have systematically studied the lengths of the legs of right triangles and the acute angles adjoining them. They have seen a pattern and described the relationships. These relationships are expressed as trigonometric functions. You can use these functions to find the length of one side if you know the length of another side and one of the acute angles. For example, the tangent function is the ratio of the side opposite an angle to the side adjacent to that angle. Demonstrate how to use the tangent formula to find the height of the ceiling. Ask one student to point their astrolabe toward an intersection of the ceiling and wall, and then take a reading of the angle. Use a scientific calculator or the tangent table (page 64) to find the tangent of the student's angle, and multiply that by the distance from the student to the wall. Then add the distance from the floor to the student's eye to obtain the approximate height of the ceiling. Check this result against the actual height of the ceiling. The answers for students sitting close to the point you are estimating may not be as accurate as the answers for students sitting farther from the point, because the tangent for large angles increases rapidly.

Distribute "How High Is the Kite?" This exercise gives students practice applying the tangent formula. The practice may be done in class or as a homework assignment. Review answers with the class. (These estimates are approximate; the answers are all rounded to the nearest ten feet: High Flyer—60 feet, Zoomer—90 feet, Birdie—610 feet, Hawk Eye—130 feet.)

Finding Distance by Pacing

Before class meets, mark the beginning and end of 50-foot or 100-foot distances and 20-meter distances in the hall or on the pavement outside. Mark off a measured distance for each group.

Ask the class how they would estimate distances that are longer than their measuring devices. Discuss their methods, then focus on

Building Kites

pacing off a distance. People who know the length of their pace can count their steps to find an unknown distance. Discuss with your students how to find the length of their own pace. Emphasize that pacing is appropriate only for estimating; students can use pacing to measure distances when accuracy to the nearest foot is sufficient. Group the students in threes or fours and distribute a copy of "Finding Your Own Pace" to each student and a calculator to each group. Bring the class to the premeasured distances and let them work. The validity of their estimates will depend on the consistency of their pacing, so they should work on developing a uniform walking style. Circulate among the groups to ask and answer questions.

When all of the students have accurately measured their paces, let them practice pacing out distances as time permits. Bring the class back together. Discuss the various methods your students used for finding the length of their paces.

Troubleshooting

The ground must be relatively level to obtain accurate measurments of distance with an astrolabe. If your students are flying their kites on a slope, they will have to take into account the slope of the hill when determining the distance from the kite to the ground. Before flying kites on a hill, brainstorm how to make the appropriate adjustments in their measurements.

Extensions

The astrolabe may be used for finding the height of buildings, trees, flagpoles, and other tall objects around the schoolground.

Students can check the accuracy of their pacing by dropping a penny on the ground, walking forward 25 paces, then turning 90°, repeating this two more times, then walking forward 25 paces. (Be sure they turn in the same direction after the same distance each time.) If their pacing and 90° turns are consistent, they will come right back to the penny!

Making an Astrolabe

Ancient astronomers used astrolabes to measure the movement of the sun, moon, planets, and stars through the heavens. You can use an astrolabe to estimate the height of very tall objects or your own kite as it flies.

You need these materials:
- copy of the astrolabe gauge
- tape
- a straw
- 12" of string
- a weight (such as a nut, washer, or heavy paper clip)
- a piece of cardboard or oaktag approximately 8" by $5\frac{1}{2}$"

Use the picture to help guide your work.
Put a check in each box as you complete the step.

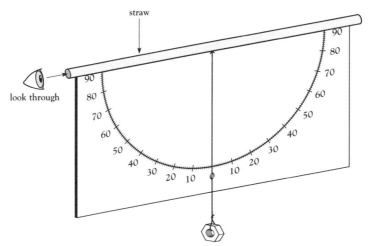

☐ Cut out the gauge.

☐ Glue the gauge along the top edge of your cardboard.

☐ Make a $\frac{1}{8}$" notch at the arrow in the center top edge of the gauge and fit one end of the string in it. Bring one inch of the string to the back of the astrolabe and tape it down well.

☐ Tie the weight to the long end of the string. This will hang free down the front side of the astrolabe.

☐ Tape the straw along the top of the astrolabe.

☐ Write your name on the back.

To use your astrolabe, look at the object through the straw, the sight, letting the string hang loose. When the object is in middle of the sight, hold the string tightly against the gauge.

Still holding the string against the astrolabe, bring it down so that you can read where the string is on the gauge. This is the number of degrees in the angle formed by the level ground and the line from your astrolabe to the object.

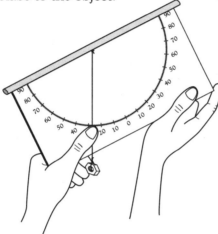

Practice taking readings of tall objects. Record you readings. Compare your readings to those of your classmates.

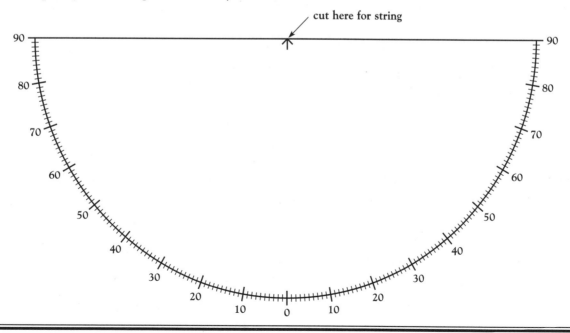

Finding Your Own Pace

When you want to know a distance but don't have a tape measure long enough, you can estimate the distance by pacing. When you pace, use a normal walking stride and count your steps. If you know the length of each pace, you can multiply by the number of paces to find the distance. For example, if your pace is two feet long and you walk 46 paces, the distance you have walked is close to 92 feet.

Your teacher has measured off a distance for you to walk.

How long is the distance? _____ feet or _____ meters

If you know the distance you walk, how will you find the length of one pace? Discuss this with your group and write your plan here.

Take turns finding the length of the pace in feet and in meters for each member in your group. You may use a calculator. Round your pace off to the nearest tenth of a foot or tenth of a meter. Show the figures you used to get the length of your pace. Be prepared to justify your work.

If you have time, practice pacing off distances until your teacher calls the class together again.

How High Is the Kite?

To measure the height of your kite with an astrolabe, make an imaginary right triangle like the one shown here.

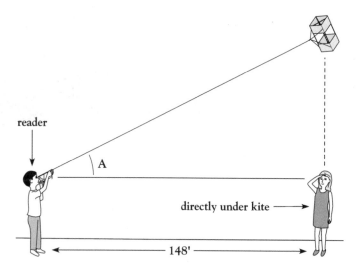

The ground is one leg of the triangle, the height of the kite is another leg, and the string is the hypotenuse. One person stands directly under the kite while another person reads the astrolabe. Then they pace off to estimate the distance between them. For example, in the drawing angle A is 35° and the distance along the ground to the kite is 148 feet. Using the tangent table (page 65) or a scientific calculator, find the tangent of angle A; tan 35 is 0.70. Multiply the tangent of angle A by the ground distance.

0.70	×	148 feet	= 103.6 feet
Tan 35°	×	ground distance to the kite	= height of kite

Now, add the distance from the ground to the astrolabe reader's eye, in this case, 5 feet.

103.6 feet + 5 feet = 108.6 feet

To show this is an approximation, 108.6 should be rounded to 110 feet.

The formula is

$$\tan A \times d + e = h$$

where
A = angle reading from the astrolabe
d = distance from astrolabe reader to directly under the kite
e = height of the reader's eye from the ground
h = height of the kite from the ground

Now use your calculator to find the height of the following kites.

Kite	Degrees of angle A	Ground distance to the kite	Height of eye	Height of kite (rounded to nearest 10 feet)
Hi-Flyer	26	115	4'6"	_____
Zoomer	48	80	5'	_____
Birdie	71	210	4'	_____
Hawk Eye	37	165	4' 9"	_____

To find the height of your kite, you need a person with an astrolabe (reader) and a person whose pace is a consistent length (pacer).

- The pacer stands directly under the kite while the reader takes a reading of angle A.
- The pacer walks to the reader, determining the distance.
- Look up the tangent of angle A.
- Use the formula $\tan A \times d + e = h$ to find the height of the kite.

Tangent Table							
Angle A	Tan A	Angle A	Tan A	Angle A	Tan A	Angle A	Tan A
1	0.02	24	0.45	47	1.07	70	2.75
2	0.04	25	0.47	48	1.11	71	2.90
3	0.05	26	0.49	49	1.15	72	3.08
4	0.07	27	0.51	50	1.19	73	3.27
5	0.09	28	0.53	51	1.24	74	3.49
6	0.11	29	0.55	52	1.28	75	3.73
7	0.12	30	0.58	53	1.33	76	4.01
8	0.14	31	0.60	54	1.38	77	4.33
9	0.16	32	0.63	55	1.43	78	4.70
10	0.18	33	0.65	56	1.48	79	5.15
11	0.19	34	0.68	57	1.54	80	5.67
12	0.21	35	0.70	58	1.60	81	6.31
13	0.23	36	0.73	59	1.66	82	7.12
14	0.25	37	0.75	60	1.73	83	8.14
15	0.27	38	0.78	61	1.80	84	9.51
16	0.29	39	0.81	62	1.88	85	11.43
17	0.31	40	0.84	63	1.96	86	14.30
18	0.33	41	0.87	64	2.05		
19	0.34	42	0.90	65	2.15		
20	0.36	43	0.93	66	2.25		
21	0.38	44	0.97	67	2.36		
22	0.40	45	1.00	68	2.48		
23	0.42	46	1.04	69	2.61		